AQÜITÍN

ENVIRONMENTAL EDUCATIVE MAGAZINE

OF WATER AND NATURE FOR CHILDREN

No 2

AUTHOR:Lic Yolanda Ma Jorge Besteiro
TRANSLATER:Lic José M. Ramos Hernández
Lic Yolanda F. Rodríguez Toledo

Index of Sections and Topics:

No 1-Curiosities about the planet earth. "Did you know ..."? The availability of water in Spain ...

No 2-Recommendations. "Do the best for everyone." Measures to save water.

No 3- Story based on real events. "Hienn and the earthquake in Java".

No.4-Dare to write with melody on themes of nature. Free Verses.

No.5-Learn and know the environment in which we live. Microorganisms present in water.

No.6- Word soup. "Learn by playing."

No.7- Concepts to learn.

No.8- Announcements and Information. "Get update". Earthquake in Java. Consequences of the passage of the Tsunami in India. Difficulties in two schools in Argentina.

Water is a common good for all.

Section 1 Curiosities about planet earth.

The apparent abundance of water in the world has given the impression, in the past, that it was an inexhaustible good. It was also the cheapest natural resource; in most regions water was free. All this has led the man to squander it.

Did you know that it has been estimated that a human being needs an average of 50 liters of water per day to drink, cook, wash, cultivate, sanitize. But the right to water, basic for any creature, is beginning to reach millions of people drop by drop.

In the 1st issue of Aqüitín we tell you that the distribution of water on the planet is irregular, being (97%) in the oceans and that only 3% of the water is fresh, of which we can use only part of it. of this because it is in the form of ice, so that the water available for human consumption is only 10 million km3.

Spain, as it has a semi-arid climate and also has a relatively low and irregular average rainfall, is not without difficulties with the availability of water for human consumption, the climate and poor management have an impact on the uneven distribution of this source of life and its infinite uses by man in our country.

In the peninsula, rivers collect about 106,000 hm3 per year, of which man can only use just over 50,000 hm3 per year thanks to the existence of reservoirs.

This availability is higher than the average for the European Union, however, there are still problems as it is distributed very unevenly and some dry areas have a shortage of water.

Did you know that ... the areas of Mediterranean climate Catalonia, the Valencian Country, Murcia, Andalusia, the Balearic Islands, as well as the Canary Islands, are the areas where rainfall has a

smaller volume; highlighting, on the peninsula, the Segura basin with an average rainfall of only 350 mm per year.

While, for example, the northern basins, with humid climate, have an average of 1350 mm per year.

As you will understand, the situation of lack of water is a global evil, although the causes are so dissimilar throughout the terrestrial sphere.

Section 2 Recommendations. "Do the best for everyone"

<u>Tips to save water:</u>

Aqüitín cares about everyone, not only children must learn to use water efficiently but they must also teach their parents since many times due to habit, lack of time or ignorance, adults neglect these aspects so necessary that, if they have them in mind, they benefit everyone.

1. Only use the dishwasher at its maximum capacity.
2. Do not use the jet to wash the vegetables, as a lot of liquid is wasted. It is preferable that you use a container where you wash them all together. Then you can use the water that I use to water the plants.

3. Do not use the well as a wastebasket, as 30 liters of water are used for each discharge. Throw away ashes, fluff and others waste in the containers designated for that purpose.

4. Plan your laundry. For each load in the washing machine, 200 liters of water are used, so it is better to wait until you have enough clothes to fill it. With the right amount of detergent, you spend less rinsing and take care of the environment. If the final water does not have soap, you can use it to water the plants or wash the floors.

5. Turn off the tap while soaping yourself, bathing, shaving or brushing your teeth.

6. Do not water the garden during the hottest hours, the water evaporates

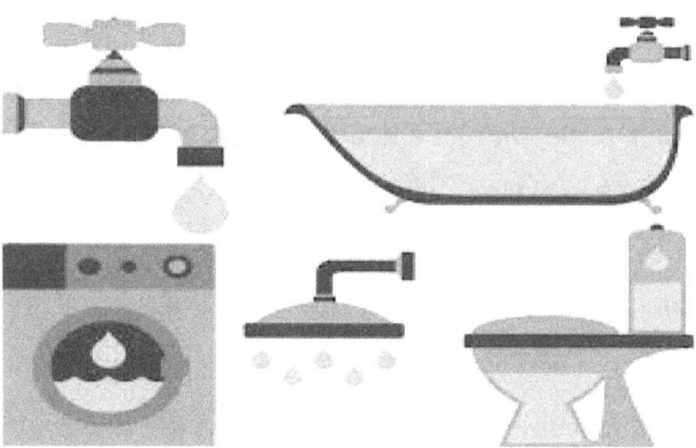

Section 3. Story

"Hienn and the earthquake in Java".

One day in May when everyone was asleep, unexpectedly the agony began, it was 5:55 in the morning when a strong shudder was heard. Hienn's parents, rested after a long day of troubles and clear roads with comings and goings through time. Days of adventures that had no end when it comes to finding water and food for the little ones in the house.

The tranquility of the picturesque town of Nogosari was suddenly interrupted by sweeping away everything it found, a huge wave of flying objects and strong wind with cloudy air that dragged a line of brick houses along an entire immense hill with extensive vegetation. An earthquake measuring 6.2 on the Richter scale with its epicenter a few kilometres from Hienn's house were invading the town noisily.

A whole chain of houses was dragged and lifted and then dropped like a manure gale, no matter how solid the foundations were, all kinds of pieces of wood rubble, pieces of inserted bricks, walls whole, windows ripped out.

All masked with trees entangled with each other, they seemed captive prey of that incredible and enormous force that had come at that moment, it is not known from where.

All the people who could fled with their clothes on, because there was no time for more, but you moved quickly, you were dragged with the rubble of garbage and all those tangled masses of trees and rubbish that were destroying everything that stood in the way.

Hienn got up as soon as he could, he was a light sleeper and had to protect his younger brother, while his desperate mother took by the arm the youngest of the five brothers, who had it not been for the speed of his mother would not save his life since in less than three minutes the house had been completely destroyed.
The speed with which everything was moving was impressive. People ran like crazy and cries of despair and panic could be heard and another neighboring family waited from the top floor of a market astonished seeing how the force of the wind also dragged water and hit a wall very close to the child.

The people of the village did not know what to do or where to go, they climbed where they could or believed they could not be touched. Hienn managed to escape with his mother and siblings, but lost sight of his father.
Some dozens of people disappeared that day, some carried away by the wind, others were crushed by objects in the attempt to flee and to flee, and many others who had no time to do anything else and were caught in the gale.

Hienn's mother and his little brothers were crying in fear and anguish, he hugged them with strength and sang a song that he learned as a child that according to his father gave encouragement and calmed the spirit of the wind. The impotence of the lost and not only his things, which despite his poverty had a few picture books with illustrations aged by time but which for him were his most precious treasure.

Few children had those books and although they were old, they were his and he learned letters from his father, since his mother could never go to school. His books flew through the air until they disappeared from the horizon and with sadness, he saw his few opportunities to continue learning lost forever. Like forever ... he thought, that he would be in that endless line of things going by at full speed banging on the roof of a house that he could barely stand in front of where he was hiding with his family.
It seems that that would never be satisfied dragging clothes and trunks of all kinds. As if he indulged in devouring whatever was found. He buried entire walls and the streets were raised in parts, divided into many pieces.

Hienn in his bravery as a young child rushed to shake hands with an old woman who was trying to hold on to the door, the boy held the old woman as strong as he could and with great effort and gathering of his strength rescued her and put her to safety, without thinking at any time that he could have lost his life in the attempt.

The survivors felt powerless they had lost everything they had been building their entire lives. Their houses were swimming back to the sea two days later, with everything that the wind had swept away with them and the vibrating and shocking movements that ripped the houses from the ground.

The remote town of Java had been completely destroyed, thousands of homes devastated, families disunited by the catastrophe, schools collapsed and scattered like ashes. Nothing was left for these people. Hienn did not understand why these things happened and asked his God very quietly, if he had done something that would have displeased him enough to cause such a disaster.

Her mother caressed him and held him against her chest, letting the tears flow that could not be stopped even because the child was looking at her, her feeling of desolation and helplessness was stronger in her, invading her to the limit of not knowing what to do or say. The poor thing had no words of comfort for her eldest son, only 10 years old.

Hienn hugged him tightly and, one by one, taking his brothers by the hands, they went down from the second floor to the roof of a market where they had taken refuge, although they had been injured and were soaked because the water tanks broke in the disaster. at least they had saved their lives, many did not suffer the same fate.

Many people in Nogosari never saw any of their relatives again, three out of four people suffered at least minor injuries, even those who saved their lives had been devastated by the damage of this misfortune. Many entire families disappeared and those that remained were left with the aftermath of this tragedy.

Nogosari was surrounded for several days and weeks by bamboo beds and multiple amounts of ropes were needed to secure a place to sleep in the sunshine of the days that followed.

Because life goes on and they can't give up. They have to fight for themselves and for the little ones who depend immensely on their loved ones to get ahead.

People were thirsty and tired and hungry with nothing to drink or put in their mouths, but the boy did not allow them to drink water from the puddles that had formed. His father

He had explained in his books that this water was not good, when it remained stagnant without movement it was the perfect food for microbes, but not everyone paid attention and removed the water from the puddles to quench the thirst that was masked with the silt and turned light brown.

Some began in the days afterward to feel unending stomach discomforts, but Hienn's family was patient and endured longer, and all those who followed his advice and that of his late father remained upright and healthy until the arrival of the surprise help.

Hienn and his family were fortunate like many of the survivors of the earthquake because days later the birds appeared from the sky that brought the salvation of those days and that of many more because it took a lot of strength, will and help to do everything again and build the houses and schools and build everything as it was before the misfortune occurred.

Hope began to show in the eyes of Hienn and his brothers when they saw that people who had nothing to do with their lives encouraged them and helped them with food, kitchen equipment, clothing and food. Above all, with clean water that despite so much running water they did not have enough clean water to drink or wash.

Java breathed deeply and nourished himself with new hopes, he counted on the strength of good, hope in children and young people and all the good of the people who helped them. But above all they had the certainty that life went on for them.

Earthquake: a natural phenomenon that produces vibrations of the earth's surface generated by a sudden and abrupt movement of the earth's inner layers (crust and mantle).

THE END

Section 4. Free Verses.

From Aquitín we encourage you to participate by writing your own rhymes on the theme of water and nature.

"Living nature"

The earth gives us food
without great impediments.
Let's take care of our plants
Let's dance while she sings
the rain on our window panes.

The earth rages
The fury of the sea appears.
Tidal waves and hurricanes
tsunamis and volcanoes.
Let's take care of our skies
with love and much zeal.

The planet loudly cries out
let's unite who loves us.
Let's all dance together
and we will hear the waves of the sea.
Let's make the world again
without hesitation for a second.

The spring does not run out
we will take care of every drop,
we can all together
pollute we must not
The whole earth comes alive
with great tenderness he pampers us.

The sun and the moon smile
the earth and the children laugh.
Let's take care of our plants
Let's dance while she sings
the rain on the windows
of our windows.

Section 5.

**Learn and know the environment in which we live.**

The problem of water use in the world is increasing, especially because the economic situation of many countries in the world transcends poverty levels, one of the essential parameters that determine this is precisely the availability of water by the population.

The water used for human consumption has to have a series of essential requirements for it to have the required quality. Not all the water that is available can be used for human consumption.

It is known that organisms of various species can be found in fresh water, however their existence causes damage to health, so none of them can be present in water for human consumption, that is why before being used for consumption, it is necessary to treat it to eliminate harmful particles and organisms and finally be able to be distributed through pipes to your home, so that you can consume it without any problem or risk to health.

Of the organisms present in the water, the so-called <u>microorganisms</u> play a considerable role due to their diversity and abundant presence in the water, among them we have bacteria, viruses, algae and protozoa.

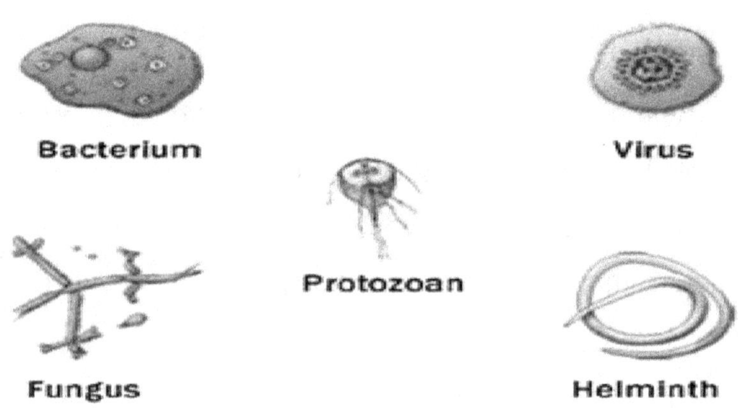

<u>Bacteria</u>: Unicellular microorganism without a nucleus defined by a membrane. They can be the cause of diseases such as typhus, cholera, venereal diseases, etc. They belong to the kingdom of protists and are only visible under a microscope because of their small size. They can also be found in water living in man and animals.

<u>Algae</u>: They are eukaryotic microorganisms and within these the simplest ones exist those that contain chlorophyll, generally they are found in waters exposed to the sun. They have a characteristic that differentiates them and that is that they do not need other living organisms to obtain food or energy.

Protozoa: They are mostly unicellular microorganisms, although they can form colonies, their cells are eukaryotic and are microscopic for the most part. They are found in waters of various characteristics (oceans, lakes, rivers, lagoons). They are also found in animals and man (some of these are pathogenic and cause malaria, sleeping sickness, amoebic dysentery, etc.

Viruses: Of the microorganisms present in water, they are the smallest, they can be more or less complex depending on their structural composition. All are parasites, invading host cells and causing them to produce more viruses.

Waterborne diseases:

Water can transmit enteric (intestinal) diseases, product of contact with human or animal waste. The most important water diseases are produced by: Bacteria, Viruses, Protozoa. Examples of bacteria, viruses and protozoa.

a) Bacteria: Shigella, Salmonella and Escherichia.

b) Viruses: microorganisms related to Hepatitis and Gastroenteritis, Coronaviruses. c) Protozoa: Giardia Lambia, Entamoeba Histolytica.

Diseases are transmitted in many ways, not only through water, but also by not washing hands well, or not washing fruits and vegetables, among many other ways that we will learn in future issues of AQÜiTÍN.

Section 6. Word soup

Order the words included in the soup accordingly. Choose one of them and make your own puzzle with three related words. AQÜITÍN will do it with these:

Microorganisms Cholera Health

Water Earthquakes Bacteria

Protozoa Virus Algae

Unicellular Prokaryotes Parasites

Section 7. Concepts to learn.

<u>Oxygen</u>: Oxygen is a chemical element, its symbol is represented by the letter O. In its most frequent molecular form, O2, it is a colorless, odorless and tasteless gas at room temperature.

<u>Odorless:</u> means it does not smell of anything

<u>Tasteless:</u> it means that it does not taste of anything.

<u>Colorless</u>: means it has no color.

Of the gases in the atmosphere, oxygen appears in 20% of the composition of the earth's atmosphere. It is the most abundant element in the earth's crust and in the oceans, forming part of the water, and the second in the atmosphere (about 20%).

<u>What does single-celled organisms mean?</u>

Unicellular are organisms composed of a single cell. Examples of organisms unicellular are bacteria, protists, and certain algae and fungi.
Some algae and fungi are multicellular, but have single-celled reproductive organs.

Unicellular organisms are considered primitive due to their low complexity compared to multicellular organisms.

Microorganisms: they are very small organisms that cannot be seen with the naked eye by the human eye, you need a microscope to see them. They are also called organisms, but it is not a correct term, because organisms can be larger or small.

Bacteria and viruses are microorganisms that we need a microscope to see. Some protozoa are also very small and cannot be seen with the naked eye.

Cholera: It is an infectious disease caused by a microbe called cholera vibrio.

The microorganism settles in the intestines of people and is eliminated through fecal matter.
Therefore, people infected with this microorganism when they go to the toilet in their feces, which then go to rivers, contaminate water and food.

Infectious: means that it infects and infects.

Spread: it means that it can be transmitted to another, that is, hitting the disease on another living being.

When we leave the bathroom, it is necessary to wash our hands well with soap and water, it is an essential hygiene rule that we must assume in our lives as something routine, but by routine it means less important.

We already know that hygiene is essential to avoid contracting diseases and then infecting to others.

With our hands we touch everything, the toilet flushing device, the walls, etc. Therefore, it is a priority to be very rigorous with our hygiene, both so as not to get sick and not to make others sick.

Have you seen a river with very dirty water and an unpleasant smell?

Well, those rivers are contaminated with organic waste, and among these, fecal bacteria. And all the animals that drink from those waters will get sick.

They will be spread by drinking water or eating food contaminated with fecal matter or vomiting that contains the choleric vibrio. In addition, insects such as flies and cockroaches can facilitate the transmission of the disease.

Section 8 Find Out and Update.

According to information published in the press by UNEP, there are 31 countries that completely lack access to clean water sources. One of every four people does not reach pure water and more than five million people die every year from contaminated water.

Hence, from Aqüitín we invite all girl and boy readers from their home and school environments to collaborate in this regard to save water and teach their parents that they educate themselves by example. We count on the support of all of you who will continue this work tomorrow and will inherit our shortcomings. That is why we need everyone.

Nature needs us and this is not the time to postpone this task.

In the 1st issue of Aqüitín we tell you what a tsunami was and about its consequences in India, because now we keep you informed of the events that continue to occur after the tragedy that occurred in that place and the problems that are being generated through the water where the floods caused by the tsunami in India the main threat is stagnant water.

"Stagnant water can be as deadly as moving water," said Carol Bellamy, Executive Director of the United Nations Children's Fund (UNICEF) in 2007, "Floods contaminate water systems, leaving people with few options except to use contaminated surface water. Under these conditions, people have a hard time protecting themselves from cholera, diarrhoea and other deadly diseases.

Children, who make up at least one third of the total population in the worst affected countries, are especially vulnerable to waterborne diseases.

Water purification tablets and oral rehydration salts to combat diarrhea they are part of the first UNICEF dispatch to the worst affected areas of Sri Lanka.

The consequences of the Tsunami in India could be even greater. The number of victims may not be limited to those who were washed away by the waves.

Contamination of drinking water resources and overloading of health care services can lead to the spread of disease.

Children affected in the tsunami zone have diseases that are directly related to the prevention and treatment of malaria, diseases related to the lack of drinking water (cholera, dysentery, diarrhea), measles, tetanus and respiratory diseases.

Malaria and dengue are epidemics that, in the current situation, with stagnant waters, favors the reproduction of these mosquitoes.

-Know about the disaster caused by an earthquake in Java.

Image published by UNICEF 48 hours after the earthquake in Java in the 2006 year.

In Indonesia, the earthquake that occurred in the middle of the year killed 75% of the population of Java. The invaluable help of UNICEF saved thousands of lives by alleviating the thirst and hunger of those days, as well as health aid. Thousands of families were left without homes and schools.

-Not only are there difficulties with water supply in Africa and India, the underprivileged population of America is also a victim of water scarcity in some cases or its mismanagement, especially children are the biggest victims.

-In june of year 2007, during the development of the face-to-face part of the International Master in Sustainable Water Engineering that is held in the Seville country relevant data were known about the water problem in some disadvantaged areas in Argentina.

The situation in question was revealed by students of the master, who work and propose solutions to solve some of these incidences of lack of management and sanitary precariousness that the population of these areas suffer.

The region that appears in the images below lacks potable water and has wells contaminated with arsenic in existence.

Images of two schools in El Barrial and Piedrita Blanca where children cannot access water for no there is any supply in its facilities. Schools Without Provision of Drinking Water or Electric Power in a town in Argentina.

Domingo Faustino Sarmiento School in El Barrial

Jorge Luis Borges School in Piedrita Blanca

Neither of these two schools has water supplies.

Children cannot use the sanitary facilities during their stay in their school activities as these are precarious or unfinished on 2007.

We trust that by today these will have been resolved.

It is necessary that children in schools receive a good education, but it is also a priority to ensure that their basic needs are taken care of, including drinking water and sanitation. These aspects are more than fundamental for everyone, and especially for children in the control of their hand and face hygiene.

<u>**Consulted bibliography**</u>

-Perspectivas del medio Ambiente Mundial 2000. PNUMA. Ed. Mundi.. 2000.

-Vivendi Environment. Annual Report 2000.

-Pictures of the schools in Las Piedritas. Argentina. Donated by Argentine students to the TAR group. University of Seville during the Water Engineering Congress "Sed Cero Ya". Sevilla.2005.

<u>**COMING SOON:**</u>

We will learn more about microorganisms and the meaning of epidemics and pandemics we will talk about the Coronavirus Cov 19.

Translaters:

- Lic José M. Ramos Hernández
  Graduated at the University in Education Biology. Researcher Writer of Literacy of Divulgation Scientific. Member of the Society Speleology and Zoology from Cuba and Dragonfly Society of the Americas (DSA), USA The Bat Conservation International (BCI), USA.

- Lic Yolanda F. Rodríguez Toledo
  Degree in Sociocultutal Studies Writer and Poet Prestigious. Esp. Integrated Management System and Quality Management.
  Metrology and Standarization

"It *is not a dream, we can achieve it water for everyone*"